I0800082

BEHOLD, WHAT WONDER!

A 30-Day Advent Journal

Friendship Press®

Copyright © 2023 by Friendship Press

All rights reserved.

No part of this book may be reproduced or utilized in any form or by any means, electronic or mechanical, or by any information storage and retrieval system, without written permission from the publisher.

Friendship Press
P.O. Box 117
Wyncote, PA 19095

Scripture quotations are taken from the New Revised Standard Version Updated Edition. Copyright © 2021 National Council of Churches of Christ in the United States of America. Used by permission. All rights reserved worldwide.

Library of Congress Catalog-in-Publication data available upon request

ISBN (hardcover): 978-1-961088-18-4

Verse selection and prompts by Heidi Hyland Mann
Cover and interior design by Laurie Ingram

Typesetting by Integra Software Services Pvt. Ltd.
Printed in the United States of America

About This Journal

Each *NRSVue Bible Journal* is offered with the hope that you will be inspired by your encounter with scripture and that journaling becomes a helpful part of your devotional journey.

The undated pages allow you to write at your own pace, with scripture passages and thoughtful writing prompts placed at regular intervals for you to meditate on, pray over, and write about as the Spirit moves you.

In this volume, the timeless story of Jesus's birth is recounted in thirty beautiful excerpts drawn largely from Luke and Matthew. The prompts encourage you to reflect on the miracle that is 'God with us', and to write your own story during this special season.

date

JOHN 1:1-5

In the beginning was the Word, and the Word was with God, and the Word was God. He was in the beginning with God. All things came into being through him, and without him not one thing came into being. What has come into being in him was life, and the life was the light of all people. The light shines in the darkness, and the darkness did not overtake it.

date

In the Gospel of John, Jesus is "the Word." What does the poetry of this passage say to you?

date

JOHN 1:14

And the Word became flesh and lived among us, and we have seen his glory, the glory as of a father's only son, full of grace and truth.

date

What does it mean to you that Jesus "lived among us" and is "full of grace and truth"?

date

date

date

LUKE 1:26-29

In the sixth month the angel Gabriel was sent by God to a town in Galilee called Nazareth, to a virgin engaged to a man whose name was Joseph, of the house of David. The virgin's name was Mary. And he came to her and said, "Greetings, favored one! The Lord is with you." But she was much perplexed by his words and pondered what sort of greeting this might be.

date

Have you ever been greeted in a strange way by someone you didn't recognize? What did they say? How did you react?

date

date

date

LUKE 1:30-34

The angel said to her, "Do not be afraid, Mary, for you have found favor with God. And now, you will conceive in your womb and bear a son, and you will name him Jesus. He will be great and will be called the Son of the Most High, and the Lord God will give to him the throne of his ancestor David. He will reign over the house of Jacob forever, and of his kingdom there will be no end." Mary said to the angel, "How can this be, since I am a virgin?"

date

Think of a time when someone told you that you would or could do something great. What was your response?

date

LUKE 1:35-37

The angel said to her, “The Holy Spirit will come upon you, and the power of the Most High will overshadow you; therefore the child to be born will be holy; he will be called Son of God. . . . For nothing will be impossible with God.”

date

What encouragement and strength does the saying "Nothing is impossible with God" give you?

date

date

date

LUKE 1:38

Then Mary said, "Here am I, the servant of the Lord; let it be with me according to your word." Then the angel departed from her.

date

Have you ever said "yes" to God in an intentional way? What was that like? What resulted?

date

date

date

LUKE 1:39-45

In those days Mary set out and went with haste to a Judean town in the hill country, where she . . . greeted Elizabeth. . . . And Elizabeth was filled with the Holy Spirit and exclaimed with a loud cry, "Blessed are you among women, and blessed is the fruit of your womb. And why has this happened to me, that the mother of my Lord comes to me? . . . And blessed is she who believed that there would be a fulfillment of what was spoken to her by the Lord."

date

Is there an older relative, friend, or mentor who celebrates you? Write about (and maybe to) that person.

date

LUKE 1:46-50

And Mary said,
"My soul magnifies the Lord,
and my spirit rejoices in God my Savior,
for he has looked with favor on the lowly state of his servant.
Surely from now on all generations will call me blessed,
for the Mighty One has done great things for me,
and holy is his name;
indeed, his mercy is for those who fear him
from generation to generation."

date

What words of praise for God are in your heart today? Write them—or sing them!

date

date

date

LUKE 1:51-55

"[The Mighty One] has shown strength with his arm;
he has scattered the proud in the imagination of their hearts.
He has brought down the powerful from their thrones
and lifted up the lowly;
he has filled the hungry with good things
and sent the rich away empty.
He has come to the aid of his child Israel,
in remembrance of his mercy,
according to the promise he made to our ancestors,
to Abraham and to his descendants forever."

date

Mary understood her pregnancy with the Son of God to be part of God's deep care for marginalized people. What response does this prompt in you?

date

date

date

MATTHEW 1:18-19

Now the birth of Jesus the Messiah took place in this way. When his mother Mary had been engaged to Joseph, but before they lived together, she was found to be pregnant from the Holy Spirit. Her husband Joseph, being a righteous man and unwilling to expose her to public disgrace, planned to divorce her quietly.

date

Have you ever learned news that shocked you and threatened to overturn some important plans for your life?

date

MATTHEW 1:20-21

But just when he had resolved to do this, an angel of the Lord appeared to him in a dream and said, "Joseph, son of David, do not be afraid to take Mary as your wife, for the child conceived in her is from the Holy Spirit. She will bear a son, and you are to name him Jesus, for he will save his people from their sins."

date

Have you ever received a direct message from God? If so, reflect on that. If not, how do you imagine such a message might come?

date

date

date

MATTHEW 1:22-23

All this took place to fulfill what had been spoken by the Lord
through the prophet:
"Look, the virgin shall become pregnant and give birth to a son,
and they shall name him Emmanuel,"
which means, "God is with us."

date

What does the statement "God is with us" mean to you?

date

date

date

MATTHEW 1:24-25

When Joseph awoke from sleep, he did as the angel of the Lord commanded him; he took her as his wife but had no marital relations with her until she had given birth to a son, and he named him Jesus.

date

Have you ever followed through on a decision despite the disapproval of others? What gave you the determination to do so?

date

LUKE 2:1-3

In those days a decree went out from Caesar Augustus that all the world should be registered. This was the first registration and was taken while Quirinius was governor of Syria. All went to their own towns to be registered.

date

How have government policies and powers affected your life, for good or ill?

date

date

date

LUKE 2:4-5

Joseph also went from the town of Nazareth in Galilee to Judea, to the city of David called Bethlehem, because he was descended from the house and family of David. He went to be registered with Mary, to whom he was engaged and who was expecting a child.

date

Reflect on a trip you were required to take. What uncertainty was involved? Was any aspect of it positive as well?

date

date

date

LUKE 2:6

While they were there, the time came for her to deliver her child.

date

Have you ever experienced a medical emergency while away from home? What happened?

date

LUKE 2:7

And she gave birth to her firstborn son and wrapped him in bands of cloth and laid him in a manger, because there was no place in the guest room.

date

Older Bible versions read, "no room in the inn." How does "guest room" change this verse for you?

date

date

date

LUKE 2:8

Now in that same region there were shepherds living in the fields, keeping watch over their flock by night.

date

Shepherds were low-wage "essential workers." What is your, or your family's, experience with work of this nature?

date

date

date

LUKE 2:9

Then an angel of the Lord stood before them, and the glory of the Lord shone around them, and they were terrified.

date

Imagine being one of the shepherds who experienced this. What are you seeing, hearing, thinking, feeling?

date

LUKE 2:10-12

But the angel said to them, “Do not be afraid, for see, I am bringing you good news of great joy for all the people: to you is born this day in the city of David a Savior, who is the Messiah, the Lord. This will be a sign for you: you will find a child wrapped in bands of cloth and lying in a manger.”

date

When has a newborn baby been for you a sign of hope?

date

date

date

LUKE 2:13-14

And suddenly there was with the angel a multitude
of the heavenly host, praising God and saying,
"Glory to God in the highest heaven,
and on earth peace among those whom he favors!"

date

What makes you praise God? What words or actions do you use to do so?

date

date

date

LUKE 2:15-16

When the angels had left them and gone into heaven, the shepherds said to one another, "Let us go now to Bethlehem and see this thing that has taken place, which the Lord has made known to us." So they went with haste and found Mary and Joseph and the child lying in the manger.

date

What would be such good news that it would make you drop everything to go see it for yourself?

date

LUKE 2:17-18

When they saw this, they made known what had been told them about this child, and all who heard it were amazed at what the shepherds told them.

date

When you have good news to share, who do you tell first? What sort of news would you be anxious to share even with strangers?

date

date

date

LUKE 2:19-20

And Mary treasured all these words and pondered them in her heart. The shepherds returned, glorifying and praising God for all they had heard and seen, just as it had been told them.

date

How do you hold onto memories you treasure?

date

date

date

MATTHEW 2:1-2

In the time of King Herod, after Jesus was born in Bethlehem of Judea, magi from the east came to Jerusalem, asking, "Where is the child who has been born king of the Jews? For we observed his star in the east and have come to pay him homage."

date

Describe a "seeking" journey you have taken. At the outset, did you know where you were going, or was it revealed little by little along the way?

date

MATTHEW 2:3-6

When King Herod heard this, he was frightened, and all Jerusalem with him, and calling together all the chief priests and scribes of the people, he inquired of them where the Messiah was to be born. They told him, "In Bethlehem of Judea, for so it has been written by the prophet:

'And you, Bethlehem, in the land of Judah,
  are by no means least among the rulers of Judah,
for from you shall come a ruler
  who is to shepherd my people Israel.'"

date

Reflect on a time you or someone else—or something—was thought to be too small or insignificant for a certain task, but in fact played a big, important role.

date

date

date

MATTHEW 2:7-8

Then Herod secretly called for the magi and learned from them the exact time when the star had appeared. Then he sent them to Bethlehem, saying, “Go and search diligently for the child, and when you have found him, bring me word so that I may also go and pay him homage.”

date

Herod's actual intent was to kill Jesus. Later, the magi are warned by an angel not to return to the king. Have you ever recognized someone's ill intent and taken steps to prevent it?

date

date

date

MATTHEW 2:9-10

When they had heard the king, they set out, and there, ahead of them, went the star that they had seen in the east, until it stopped over the place where the child was. When they saw that the star had stopped, they were overwhelmed with joy.

date

Are you ever able to stargaze away from artificial light? What does that experience mean to you?

date

MATTHEW 2:11

On entering the house, they saw the child with Mary his mother, and they knelt down and paid him homage. Then, opening their treasure chests, they offered him gifts of gold, frankincense, and myrrh.

date

If you could give Jesus physical gifts in person, what would those be?

date

date

date

GALATIANS 4:4-7

But when the fullness of time had come, God sent his Son, born of a woman, born under the law, in order to redeem those who were under the law, so that we might receive adoption as children. And because you are children, God has sent the Spirit of his Son into our hearts, crying, "Abba! Father!" So you are no longer a slave but a child, and if a child then also an heir through God.

date

What does it mean to you that because of Jesus's birth, you have been "adopted" into the family of God and are an heir of all God's goodness?

date

date

date